D1093514

HINDU
PROVERBS
AND WISDOM

Compiled by Narendra K. Sethi

Illustrated by Jeff Hill

PETER PAUPER PRESS
Mount Vernon, N. Y.

HINDU
PROVERBS
AND
WISDOM

HINDU PROVERBS
AND WISDOM

A fool is honored in his house; a merchant is honored in his town; a king is honored in his state; a wise man is honored in all lands.

Each man is the sole guardian of his own honor.

The village says "go"; the cemetery says "come."

Can the stomach be filled by holding in the breath?

Life is a river; virtue is its bathing place; truth is its water; moral convictions are its banks; mercy is its wave. In such a pure river, bathe.

Vain is rain on the ocean; vain is food for a full man; vain is charity for him capable of earning; vain is a lamp at noon.

Judge a woman not by her charms but her qualities; judge a man not by his birth but his conduct; judge a scholar not by his learning but his achievement; and judge a merchant not by his fortune but by his understanding.

———

A peach in the paw of a monkey; a pearl in the snout of a swine.

———

No quarrel with silence; no qualms with vigilance.

———

Knowledge begets humility; humility produces worthiness; worthiness encourages wealth; wealth sustains religion; and all together they create happiness.

———

Who fails to eat is undone; who fails in business is undone; who fails in court is undone; who fails with his mother-in-law is undone.

———

Eat fire and your mouth will burn; live on credit and your pride will burn.

Kings speak but once; scholars speak but once; daughters are given in marriage but once. These things, done but once, are done once for all.

———

Who on earth will the beauty of a damsel not subdue?

———

The mind of man is the root of both bondage and release.

———

What is *Dharma*? Kindness. What is happiness? Being free from disease. What is friendship? Being good to others. What is learning? The ability to discriminate.

———

Who is honored in adversity?

———

All entrusted to others is grief; all undertaken by one's self is joy.

———

No great loss to the elephant if a few grains fall, but the ant can feed its whole family with the trickle.

A drop of water falling on a red-hot iron vanishes without leaving a trace. The same drop falling on a lotus-leaf shines like a pearl. The same drop falling into an oyster becomes a pearl. Thus men who associate with the inferior, the ordinary, and the superior respond accordingly.

———

Speak like a parrot; meditate like a swan; chew like a goat; and bathe like an elephant.

———

Superiority does not follow from age but from virtue.

———

Debt, a sore, and a stain will be effaced by time.

———

Youth, abundant wealth, high birth, and inexperience: each of these is a source of ruin. What then the fate of him in whom all four are joined?

———

The desires of the poor spring up just to be destroyed.

A country deprived of its rivers is ruined; a family deprived of its learning is ruined; a woman deprived of her children is ruined.

_____

He alone is truly good who is dumb in abusing others' faults; who is blind in seeing others' women; who is lame in pursuing others' wealth.

_____

When the liberal man gives, his steward's heart breaks.

_____

A fly, a harlot, a beggar, a rat, and a gusty wind; the village-boss and the tax-collector — these seven are always annoying to others.

_____

Varied are the ways of fortune.

_____

Nobody with eyes open dares swallow a fly.

_____

Time drinks up the essence of great actions which should be quickly done but are delayed.

There are only two alternatives for noble men; either to be at the head of all, or to fade away in the forest.

Stop your thousand acts, and eat.

Fortune smiles on the stout-hearted and the self-preserving.

A friend can be won by sincerity of conduct; an enemy by prudence and power; a miser by wealth; a master by service; a Brahmin by kindness; a wife by tenderness; a relative by patience; a passionate man by praise; a fool by stories; a wise man by knowledge; a tasteful man by humor; and every one by good behavior.

The King must answer for the country's sins; the priest for the king's sins; the husband for the wife's sins; and the teacher for the disciple's sins.

An old woman makes a chaste wife.

A reasonable word of advice may come even from a child or parrot.

The miser can neither give nor enjoy his money. He merely touches it, as a eunuch touches a woman.

Among noblemen high rank is attained by knowledge; among warriors, by valor; among businessmen by grain and money; only among the poor by birth.

Our mind obeys what our fate says.

A treacherous wife would kill you and then share your pyre.

Cows learn by smelling; wise men by remembering; kings by asking; and common people by seeing.

Say, what does not good association accomplish for men?

A fool shines so long as he keeps silent.

A book, a woman and money given to others never come back. Or if they do, they come back polluted and torn.

———

Who has reached the limit of his desires?

———

The blind man distributes shares, but only to his family.

———

Milk nourishes the poison of snakes. Good counsel to the unworthy provokes rather than satisfies them.

———

Foolish is the city, and foolish is the king, where vegetables and sweetmeats both sell at a penny a pound.

———

Even a single lion can tear to pieces a herd of elephants.

———

If the priest does not come, will the new moon wait for him?

———

The joys and sorrows of a lonely man touch no one.

14

You can convince an ignorant man easily; you can convince a wise man more easily. But a man who knows a little and thinks himself to be perfect, not even *Brahma* can convince.

To serve an imprudent man is as vain as sounding a trumpet for the deaf, or holding up a mirror for the blind.

No pleasure is enjoyed without some pain.

The cake in the oven is yours; the cake in the tray is mine.

Make peace with the powerful, war with the equal; and make quick raids against the timid.

The sun is red at dawn and red at sunset. Great men are unchanged in prosperity and in distress.

May all here bathe in milk and be fruitful in children!

By the falling of a few drops of water, the pot is slowly filled. So too we may gradually acquire knowledge, virtue, and riches.

What is gain? The society of the wise. What is misery? The company of fools. What is loss? The passing away of favorable opportunity. What is perfection? Deep faith in religious tenets. Who is a hero? He who can subdue his senses. What is happiness? Residence in one's native land. And, ask the wise men, what is empire? The establishment of real authority.

How long does a gypsy's marriage last? How long does an entertainment last?

You can wake a man who is asleep, but not a man who is awake.

The teacher remained molasses, but the disciple was distilled to sugar.

In a strong position even a coward is a lion.

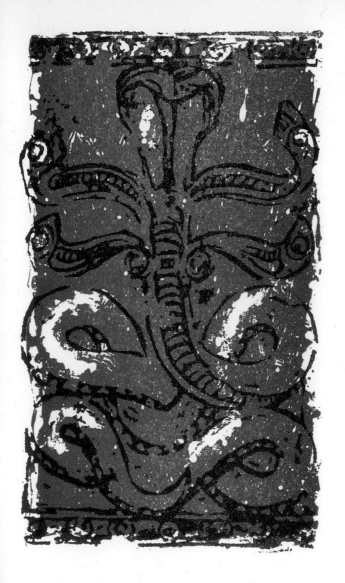

Thirst cannot be quenched by licking the lips.

_____

No matter what his caste and clan, he who remembers God will go to Him.

_____

Once you get a place to stand on, you will soon be granted a room to sit in.

_____

Fortune's dwelling-place is trade.

_____

A friend may be judged in adversity; a hero in war; an honest man in money-lending; a wife in poverty; and a relative in trouble.

_____

She is a wife who is efficient in her house; she is a wife who is fruitful in her children; she is a wife who is cheering to her family; she is a wife who is obedient to her husband.

_____

A bad wife; an undependable friend; an insolent servant; a haunted house: these mean death.

Great heat at the beginning ruins grand projects. Water, although it is cool, makes the earth fertile.

———

What can wise precepts of scripture do for one without natural wisdom? What can a mirror do for one without eyes?

———

Sorrow for a dead father lasts six months; sorrow for a dead mother for a year; sorrow for a wife until a second wife arrives; but sorrow for a dead son for ever.

———

Food provided without affection is like food offered to the dead.

———

God's most wondrous deeds: one moment sunshine; another moment shade.

———

Entertainment brings relatives, and flattery brings fortune.

———

Fall from a horse and you may be saved; fall from public respect and you are lost.

19

Cleanliness in the crow; honesty in the gambler; valor in the eunuch; learning in the drunkard; kindness in the snake; friendliness in the King: — who has ever seen or heard of such?

———

In a noble man, anger lasts for a moment; in a worldly man for two hours; in a base man for a day; and in an evil man until death.

———

He who has many enemies is like a pigeon among kites: whichever way he turns, he faces attack.

———

A fool leaves the food which awaits him, and goes to beg.

———

How far can you push a person up on a tree?

———

Money is best when acquired by one's own hands. It is not so good when inherited. It is bad when it is a brother's. It is worst when it is a woman's.

Proficiency in advising others is common. Rare is the man who himself practices the virtue he can preach.

To argue with a man of noble speech is better than to agree with a man of rude speech.

He whose time has arrived, lives not.

Learning, jewels, virtues, good habits, polite manners, sweet speech, artistry: accept them from whatever source offers.

Where the servant is without pay, the master must be without anger.

A parrot likes to be petted himself, but does not wish others to be petted.

Must you teach your grandfather how to cough?

Stick to one thing and all will come; aim at everything and all will go.

The tree may be cut back, but it grows again. The moon may wane, but it shines anew. Good men go on despite calamities.

———

What a man dreams for his projects, and what the gods decide for them, are two different things.

———

He alone lives on who gathers fame.

———

Wealth in cattle; wealth in elephants; wealth in gold; wealth in gems — all are as dust when wealth in contentment comes.

———

Every hero, from his first residence in the womb, day by day approaches Death.

———

One touch of the whip for a fine horse; one word for a noble man.

———

A great objective, indeed; but a bad road ahead.

———

Though not your kin, a friend is your best relation.

23

A roaring ocean may be crossed by a ship. A dark night may be dispelled by a lamp. A hot summer day may be cooled by a fan. A wild elephant may be captured by a goad. There is no evil in the world for which destiny has not found a remedy. But even *Brahma* cannot find a cure for the evil workings of an ignoble man.

———

One can no more make a saint of a soldier, than a bow out of a pestle.

———

He is a friend in whom there is confidence; she is a wife in whom there is pleasure.

———

Giving is in the power of the giver.

———

Better that the body remain slim than become heavy with dropsy.

———

Meditation should be done alone; study by two together; musical practice by three; traveling by four; agriculture by five; and battle by many.

Vice and virtue arise from bad and good association.

_____

Those without a leader perish; those with a childish leader perish; those with a female leader perish; those with a multitude of leaders perish.

_____

Will you worship the Sun after losing your eyes?

_____

The wicked promise and give their hands a hundred times; but who can cross a flooded river by grasping a ram's tail?

_____

Does it matter a bit if you drink milk in a dream out of a pottery cup or a golden vessel?

_____

There is no penance more effective than patience; no happiness equal to joyfulness; no disease more killing than lust; no virtue richer than humility.

_____

Who can get the better of fate?

Those who have neither wisdom, nor devotion; neither charity, nor spirituality; neither good conduct, nor morality; neither religious faith, nor pious habits — are mere useless burdens to Mother Earth, wandering over the world like the deer in human form.

———

A son should be treated as a prince for five years; as a slave for ten years; but from his sixteenth birthday, as a close friend.

———

Dependence on others brings a perpetual fast.

———

The bad man should be honored first and the good man afterwards. The feet should be washed first and the mouth afterwards.

———

When the husband has no wisdom, the wife has no pride.

———

Woman is a pot of oil; man is a burning coal. Wise men do not put oil and fire together.

Keep one God, either *Kesava* or *Siva*; one home, either town or forest; one friend, either king or hermit; one desire, a beautiful wife or a wilderness cave.

———————

Though you turn a fire over, its flame will never flow down.

———————

Everything is created with a companion that will destroy it.

———————

Teeth, hair, nails and men become worthless once removed from their proper place. A wise man sticks to his own station.

———————

If your foot slips, you may regain your balance; if your mouth slips, you cannot recall your words.

———————

Birds of different countries alight upon one tree; but at dawn, they fly their different ways. Do they feel regret or sorrow?

———————

What is gone is gone, gone.

Though the snake be small, hit him with a big stick.

———

The scorpion's poison: in his tail; the fly's poison: in his head; the snake's poison: in his fang; the bad man's poison: in his whole body.

———

A rotten tooth, a faithless servant, a wicked minister — they are best torn out by their roots.

———

Who befriends is a relation; who supports is a father.

———

A dog, even when adorned with a jeweled collar, does not show the majesty the lion has by his inherent merit.

———

The writing on the forehead can never be effaced.

———

There is no one who knows everything; there is no one who knows nothing.

———

Modesty is the embellishment of women.

He is a worthy son who brings pleasure to his parents by noble deeds; she is a worthy wife who cares for the welfare of her husband; he is a worthy friend who is unchanged by prosperity and adversity. Such a son, wife or friend come to men by good fortune alone.

———

Learn the good ways of your enemies; avoid the bad ways of your elders.

———

A rat, a buffalo, a ram, a crow, and a man of no discretion, are excluded from confidence. It is not expedient to put any trust in them.

———

Modesty is ruinous to the harlot, immodesty to the respected woman.

———

A man who misses his opportunity, and a monkey who misses his branch, cannot be saved.

———

The King is the power of the weak; tears are the power of children.

A king learns by his ears; a saint by his intellect; a beast by his nose; and a fool by his experience.

———

The man who seeks out your faults is a father; the man who seeks out your virtues is an envier.

———

A wise man should not reveal the loss of his fortune, the vices in his house, the fact that he was cheated or has been disgraced.

———

In a quarrel between bulls, it's the calf's leg that gets broken.

———

Is a lamp pleasing to the blind; a song to the deaf; or a book to the fool?

———

The wise man keeps one foot firm, and moves the other. Without making sure of your next move, do not give up your present place.

———

In a land without trees even the castor plant will be called a tree.

What formality is there in one's own home?

———

Rivers do not drink their own water. Trees do not eat their own fruit. Clouds do not swallow their own rain. What great ones have is always for the benefit of others.

———

The Earth feels no evil.

———

Trust not rivers; or animals with claws and horns; or men with weapons; or women with good looks.

———

Cuckoos do well to keep silent in the winter. When frogs are croaking, then silence is becoming.

———

For the childless, the house is empty; for the kinless the land is empty; for the blockhead, the heart is empty; for the poor, the world is empty.

———

He alone is truly worthy who supports many other lives along with his own.

If it is given with love, a mere handful is enough.

———

You should learn what you can swallow and what can swallow you.

———

A dumb man's sugar is called neither sour nor sweet.

———

"A leaf, a flower, a fruit, and water." [Said apologetically by the poor host to a rich guest.]

———

Even the gods know not in advance a woman's mind or a man's fortune; how then can we?

———

Wandering ages men; celibacy ages women. Horses age by confinement and clothes by exposure.

———

In one scale, the four *Vedas*; in the other, natural common-sense.

———

An injured foot is always stumbling into rocks.

The one-eyed love the one-eyed; the queen loves a king.

An elegant shop, but the sweets they sell are tasteless.

Money left in a woman's hands will not last long; children left in a man's hands will not live long.

The mind is depraved by the society of the ignoble. It rises to equality with equals and to distinction with the distinguished.

A wise man knows how to suit his words to the occasion; his love to the worthiness of the loved one; and his wrath to his power.

Run as far and as fast as you wish; you will reach only that which is ordained.

Learning depends on practice; intellect on previous deeds; wealth on effort; and success on good fortune.

A King is ruined by evil counsel; an ascetic by material cravings; a child by careless caresses; a Brahmin by neglected studies; a distinguished family by wicked children; moral conduct by contact with evil; modesty by drinking; crops by negligence; love by separation; friendship by indifference; property by injustice and wealth by squandering.

———

A dinner when hunger is gone; a coat when cold is gone; a wife when youth is gone; are things best done without.

———

He who is under another's thumb has no rest even in his dreams.

———

No fragrance from a withered flower. No help from a husband in a foreign land.

———

Ruin will come to be his dole who leaves the half to grasp the whole.

———

A wife is not merely mate; she is entire fate.

A little oil dropped on water, a secret entrusted to a woman, a gift presented to a noble man, learning imparted to a wise man — these spread without outside stimulus.

A good son is the light of the family.

Life is for the purpose of religion, labor, love, and salvation. If these are destroyed, what is not destroyed? If these are preserved, what is not preserved?

The python does no service; the birds do no toil; God gives them what they need.

Hold on to your luggage and walk slowly; if you don't reach there today, you will tomorrow.

Hospitality is commanded even toward an enemy who comes to your house. The tree does not withdraw its shade from the wood-cutter.

A companion is an added strength.

A wise man should forsake the friend who speaks kindly to his face but defeats his actions behind his back. Such a friend is a cup of poison with a surface layer of milk.

———

Don't try to go where your talents are not needed; what should a laundry-man do in Naked Town?

———

In water a stone gets wet but never dissolves; in the wise man's presence a fool may be pleased but never improved.

———

It is milk if it comes without asking; it is water if it comes by begging.

———

The patient does not recover health by hearing the medicine described.

———

Fortitude in adversity, moderation in prosperity; eloquence in assembly, valor in war; glory in renown, and diligence in meditation: these are the natural perfections of great men.

39

A thorn sticks into a great man and hundreds run to help; a poor man falls down a cliff and no one comes near.

———

Everyone claims relationship to the rich.

———

If you go too near, they destroy you. If you keep too far away, they do not serve you. Therefore stay neither too near nor too far away from Kings, from Fire, from Elders and from Women.

———

Only in adversity do the virtues of man reach their height. In the absence of wind, a heap of cotton is as steady as a mountain-top.

———

From a debt to one's father; from a single daughter; and from traveling a mile alone may God preserve you.

———

He who has built a house has one home; he who has built no house must share a thousand homes.

A woman's glance is like a wicked person. It attaches itself to those who cannot control their senses; it diverts the mind's concentration; it moves crookedly like a poisonous snake; and carries itself proud and lofty.

A thief, a gamester, a pickpocket, a rake, and a harlot: never trust them though they swear a thousand oaths.

Practice virtue as if death had seized you by the hair.

Whether wedded to austere meditation or to worldly pleasure; whether tied with family bonds or single and unattached; if your mind is concentrated on God, you can rejoice deeply.

God has three qualities: to give, to make others give, and to take back what He has already given.

In the absence of men all women are chaste.

Speak to please the world; eat to please yourself.

The widow's spinning-wheel, and the glutton's mouth, are always going.

He who has brought you forth; he who has invested you with the sacred thread; he who has given you instruction; he who has provided you food; he who has saved you from danger; these five are to be remembered as father.

One should avoid these six evils: lust, avarice, anger, pleasure, pride and haste; for, free of these, one may be happy.

In work a slave; in business a diplomat; in form a goddess; in intercourse a courtesan; in virtue firm as earth; in giving food like a mother: is she not a worthy wife?

A discontented Brahmin is as lost as a contented king.

The poor man's youth; the summer's sun; the winter's moon: these three pass away unenjoyed.

————

A daughter, a son-in-law, and a nephew; these three are never one's own.

————

Disease threatens enjoyment; degradation threatens reputation; rulers threaten wealth; enemies threaten strength; age threatens beauty; death threatens the body — everything has its threat. Only renunciation has no threat.

————

Joined together, even little things are strong. A mad wild elephant can be bound with a few straws if the straws are formed into a rope.

————

He who swallows is better off than he who only chews.

————

The woman who has daughters sits on a chair; the lady who has sons leans against the wall.

Inferior men do not begin undertakings for fear of difficulties. Average men begin, but desist once difficulties appear. Men of superior nature never give up until they achieve their ends, however many the difficulties that appear.

None ever died from cursing or lived from blessing.

Good food is that shared with others; good friendship is that rendering help even in adversity. Good wisdom is that doing no evil; good deeds of virtue are those done without pride.

I am come from Delhi and my brother tells me the news!

Kings, creepers, and courtesans cling to whoever stands nearest.

Mind is transitory; wealth is transitory; life is transitory; youth is transitory. He alone lives on who acquires fame.

Blackness cannot be removed from charcoal even by a hundred washings.

Like a shadow in the morning, the friendship of the ignoble man is great at first, then gradually decreases and disappears. Like a shadow in the afternoon, the friendship of the noble man is small at first, then gradually increases.

A sick man's night is as long as a mountain trail.

Spring is the strength of trees; wealth is the strength of men; beauty is the strength of women; intelligence is the strength of youth.

Where there is a noble soul, there also is God.

Even if the sun should rise in the West; even if the lotus should bloom on the mountain-top; even if fire should feel cold, the words of the wise will never fail.

Rare is he who appreciates merit. Rare is he who seeks the friendship of the poor. Rare is he who shows courage in battle. And rare indeed is he who grieves at the grief of others.

He who crows over an uncompleted work is a candidate for woe.

Slowly along the road; slowly through the forest; slowly over the mountains; slowly in doing business; slowly in giving charities; slowly indeed through all these five.

Pouring poison in a golden cup does not make it nectar.

When the wife embraces the husband without love, she has some other reason.

For the belly's sake we put on many a disguise.

With a Brahmin for minister and a bard for favorite, the Rajah is ruined.

For the good of a family, a member may be abandoned; for the good of a town, a family may be abandoned; for the good of a state, a town may be abandoned; for the good of your soul, all you own may be abandoned.

———

If the tree would not bend when green, will it bend when grown?

———

God makes the great, mean; the mean, great.

———

What is impossible is impossible. Only what is possible is possible. The cart cannot roll on water; the ship cannot sail on land.

———

Misfortune is the touchstone by which a man discovers the character of his wife, relations, and servants; and of his own strength and skill.

———

No delight like misery when it doesn't last long.

If *Brahma* wishes, will you lack for days enough in your life? If your husband wishes, will you lack for blows enough on your back?

From labor comes fruit.

A drop of water is the sea to the noble mind; the ocean is a drop of water to the wicked.

Enquire not into the origin of a saint, a river, and an old woman.

Always act as the people desire.

"O blanket, where are you?" he inquired. "Where you left me, you knave!"

Four *Vedas*; the fifth teaching is a cudgel.

What does a barren woman know of the pains of labor?

Of the six flavors, salt is the first.

The noble man, even in ignominy, cannot be deprived of noble qualities. A flaming torch may be turned downward, but its flame will rise upward.

———

Boats come on carts; carts come on boats.

———

A mean man promises and does not; a good man promises not but does.

———

For uneven ground, great swamps and dreadful hills, use an elephant; for plains use a horse; for rivers use a boat — but the foot can be used anywhere.

———

Everyone kisses the smooth cheek.

———

So long as there is food in the mouth, so long will the words be sweet.

———

These six — the peevish, the niggardly, the dissatisfied, the passionate, the suspicious, and the dependent — are always unhappy.

51

A hundred good actions are lost upon the unworthy; a hundred good words are lost upon the ignorant; a hundred good qualities are lost upon the ignoble; a hundred wise sayings are lost upon the insensible.

Be charitable according to your means.

After the stream has been crossed, what use is the boat on the other side?

Before you knew, it was difficult; once you knew, it was easy.

The bankrupt has credit only in hell.

Without asking, we get pearls; by begging, not even pennies.

Easy it is to partake of opium; but deadly is the enjoyment thereof.

Be a brother to the good; a son-in-law to the bad.

Nectar should be extracted even out of poison; a well-expressed word should be accepted even from a youth; rectitude should be acknowledged even in an enemy; and gold should be taken even out of filth.

———

You'll never get by begging what was lacking at the feast.

———

The roots of belief are always green.

———

Silence is the ornament of the illiterate, especially in the assembly of learned men.

———

Even a sheep bites the man without a stick.

———

A friend should be received with compassion; a relation with respect; a woman with compliment; and others with whatever is appropriate.

———

He who flees from an ill-governed town shall survive.

———

Big drums follow the little ones.

He who created our mouths will feed them.

Begging in a foreign land: better than stealing in your own.

The voice is the beauty of cuckoos; chastity is the beauty of women; wisdom is the beauty of the deformed; patience is the beauty of the noble.

All are naked under their loin cloth.

If your own family point their fingers at you, outsiders will point their feet.

He who is totally ignorant of literature and music is a tailless, hornless beast; that he can live without eating grass is fortunate for cattle, who thus can make a free and full use of their natural food.

The base love strife; the good love peace.

Where there is justice there is victory.

Ingenuity is needed, even to practice vice.

———

Only fortune is fruitful; neither learning nor human effort is.

———

If you clap with but one hand, will there be a sound?

———

A husband is a woman's first ornament, though he himself dress plainly. When she has no husband, she is not adorned, no matter what ornaments she wears.

———

When sugar can kill, why feed poison?

———

To keep your honor, do not ask even for water.

———

Care is flame and body is wood; others see no smoke, for the burning is within.

———

What can fall from the fallen?

———

Too great exaltation is the beginning of downfall.

Ignoble men, after obtaining favors, revert to their natural disposition. A dog's tail, after every possible anointing and bending, returns to its natural twist.

———

Offering without faith is a waste of flowers.

———

In eating and in trading, he who discards modesty wins.

———

The thunderbolt and the king's power are both dreadful. The bolt expends its fury at once; but the king strikes again and again.

———

You have a future life when your grandson plays at the door.

———

A word is medicine enough for the wise.

———

It is we who are exhausted, not the pleasures; it is we who are given, not the penances; it is we who are lost, not the time; it is we who have grown old, not the desire of gain.

The remains of a debt, of a sore, and of a fire, should not be neglected.

———

Strife is a loss, friendship a gain.

———

Although a jewel may fall in the mud, and a piece of glass be worn on the turban, yet at the time of buying and selling, glass is glass and jewel is jewel.

———

The clock strikes differently each hour.

———

If it is not to be, it will not be; if it is to be, it will be.

———

There is no village, how can there be a boundary? There is no learning, how can there be fame? There is no faith, how can there be understanding?

———

Even when the elephant sits, he is as high as the horse.

———

Innumerable maladies hide within the body.

Fortune rests on your tongue-tip; friends and relatives rest on your tongue-tip; suffering and imprisonment rest on your tongue-tip; death and life itself rest on your tongue-tip.

———

Without a wife in the house, the devil will live there.

———

Share your purse and proudly eat pottage.

———

The Sun and Moon; fire and air; heaven and earth; heart and conscience; day and night with morning and evening; are all witnesses of a man's actions.

———

A family survives by having one head, not many heads.

———

The sound of a distant drum is pleasant.

———

A good man says no slowly; a wise man says no at once.

———

See on which side the camel sits down.

A mother is divinity; a father is treasure.

———

Catch a thief at the money-box, the harlot on the bed.

———

None dies before his time though pierced by hundreds of arrows; he whose time has run out lives not though struck only by a blade of grass.

———

Only poison is the remedy of poison.

———

If you put a crow in a cage, will it talk like a parrot?

———

It is always dark just under the lamp.

———

For the broad-minded, the very universe is home.

———

To see the eclipses of Sun and Moon; to see the capture of wild elephants and snakes; and to see the poverty of the wise, is to see that the power of fate is always supreme.